**W9-ALM-457**

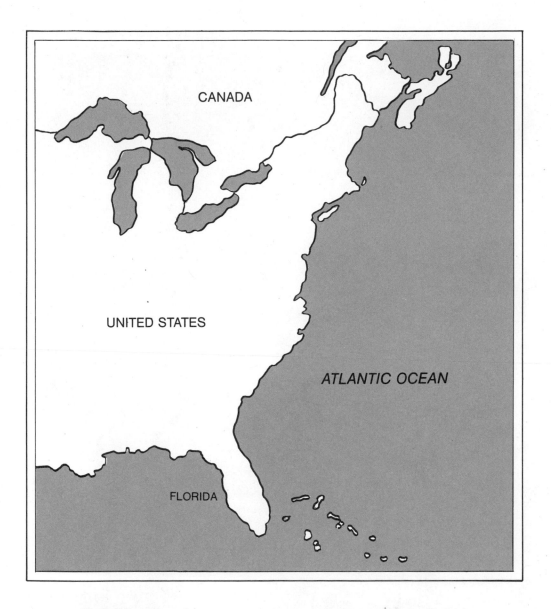

Dolphins live in oceans, seas, and rivers around the
world. Bottle-nosed dolphins are often found in the
Atlantic Ocean, off the east coast of the United
States. This story takes place in the Atlantic Ocean
and in a sea show in southern Florida.

# Doll

## Bottle-Nosed Dolphin

By Sally Glendinning

Drawings by Arabelle Wheatley

GARRARD PUBLISHING COMPANY
CHAMPAIGN, ILLINOIS

## Photo Credits

Nina Leen, Life Magazine, © Time, Inc.: p. 5
Miami Seaquarium: pp. 12, 35
Lowell Georgia/National Audubon Society Collection/
  Photo Researchers: p. 13
Russ Kinne/National Audubon Society Collection/
  Photo Researchers: pp. 16, 19
© Al Naidoff, Design Photographers International: p. 26
Peter Stackpole, Life Magazine, © Time, Inc.: pp. 31, 39
Marine World Africa/USA: p. 34 (bottom)

## Map on page 1 by Benjamin C. Blake

Library of Congress Cataloging in Publication Data

Glendinning, Sally.
    Doll: bottle-nosed dolphin.

    (Young animal adventures)
    SUMMARY: A baby dolphin that has been bitten by a
shark and rescued by two fishermen begins a life of
captivity in a salt-water sea show where she performs
tricks.
    [1. Atlantic bottlenosed dolphin—Juvenile literature.
2. Animals, Infancy of—Juvenile literature.
3. Wild animals, Captive—Juvenile literature.
4. Wild animals, Captive] I. Wheatley, Arabelle.
II. Title. III. Series.
QL737.C432G53     636′.953     80-13660
ISBN 0-8116-7501-7

# Doll: Bottle-Nosed Dolphin

The baby dolphin was born in the Atlantic Ocean on a sunny morning in May. A year had gone by since the baby's mother and father had mated, so the little dolphin had a long time to grow inside her mother's body.

She was nearly three feet long when she was born, and she weighed about 25 pounds. She looked like a dolphin doll. She was plump, cuddly, and soft. Her eyes were open, and her mouth was shaped into a smile. The tiny blowhole on top of her head was shut tight as she swam underwater by her mother's side.

5

Dolphins are usually
born tail first. As
soon as this baby is
born, the mother will
push it to the top to
breathe. Then the baby
will swim beside its
mother and the old fe-
male dolphin who helps
to care for it.

Mother Dolphin pushed the baby gently up through the water to the top, where there was air. As soon as the baby's blowhole was above the water, she breathed air in and out quickly. The baby would drown if she breathed in as much as a spoonful of water.

Mother Dolphin made soft sounds, as if she were singing to her new baby. On the other side of the baby swam an old female dolphin. She was ready to help the mother care for the little one. Father Dolphin and many other bottle-nosed dolphins swam near them.

The dolphins made whistling sounds to one another as they swam and played. They were careful to look for any sharks that might be nearby. Many of the dolphins had scars from shark bites. They didn't want a shark to hurt the new baby.

Now the baby dolphin was hungry. She swam under her mother, looking for food. The baby found a tiny opening on Mother Dolphin's underside. She put her mouth against the opening. Mother Dolphin quickly squirted some milk into the baby's mouth. Then they swam to the top to breathe in some more air.

For the first few days and nights, the baby dolphin napped, ate, and swam to the top for air. One day she napped for a minute or two with the top of her head above the water. Mother Dolphin made a crackling sound and whistled to the baby. The baby's head would be sunburned if the little one stayed above the water too long.

As the baby grew older, she began to listen to all the sounds made by the big dolphins.

This baby dolphin is drinking its mother's milk.

They talked among themselves mostly by whistling. Each dolphin had his very own whistling sound—his "name-whistle." The little dolphin tried hard to whistle, but all that came out was a tiny squeak.

Mother Dolphin patted her with a flipper. She knew it would be a long time before the little dolphin could make her own name-whistle.

9

The big dolphins also could make a series of clicking sounds. These clicks were much, much faster than the ticking of a clock. The sounds traveled a long way underwater. The dolphins could tell when the clicking sounds hit something in the water far away. They could tell whether the object was a hungry shark or a piece of wood floating by.

One day the little dolphin swam away from her mother. She became frightened, for she thought she was lost.

Mother Dolphin started to look for her baby. She found her easily by sending out clicks, first one way and then another. The sounds, traveling through the water, bounced off the baby and back to Mother Dolphin.

Then Mother scolded the little one for swimming too far away.

The little dolphin soon knew all the other dolphins. Those that swam together in her group were called a school or herd. Although they looked alike, they acted differently. There was The Hunter, who did not whistle very often. Instead, he made clicking sounds as he listened for fish. He could hear better than the others, and he liked to hunt for food even when he wasn't hungry.

Another dolphin in the school was The Fighter. He kept a sharp lookout for sharks. He seemed always to be ready for a good fight. He had a long scar on his side where a shark had bitten him.

The Talker was an old dolphin who whistled all the time. He talked about all sorts of things even when nobody listened.

The school of dolphins made a lot of noise

under the water as they swam up and down the coastline of the Atlantic Ocean. They whistled, clicked, groaned, and sputtered. The dolphins were very noisy when they played games. Father Dolphin was always the leader, for he liked to make up new games to play.

Each day, when it was time for games, he

Dolphins love to play. The one at the
left leaps high out of the water. Two
dolphins below swim on their backs.

would swim fast and leap from the water
high into the air. The others would try to do
the same. Some could leap very high. Others
could hardly get out of the water. The little
dolphin could not yet play this leaping game.

Then Father Dolphin would roll over so that
his white belly was just below the water. All

the dolphins would roll over and swim on their backs until it was time to come up for air. The little dolphin tried to swim on her back, too.

She liked it best when Father stood on his tail. He would leap from the water with a loud swishing sound and hold his body straight in the air. He balanced himself by flicking his tail back and forth in the water. None of the others could stand on their tails as long as Father did. Each day the little dolphin tried to stand on her tail, but she was not strong enough yet.

Until she was six months old, the little dolphin drank only her mother's milk. After her cone-shaped teeth began to grow, she and Mother Dolphin started to play a game of their own. Mother Dolphin would toss a bit of fish to the little dolphin, and she would catch it in her teeth. They played their game day after day until the little one finally ate a bit of fish. She liked it! After that, she often caught a small fish for herself.

One day the dolphins heard the sound of many fish swimming together. They knew from the sound underwater that a school of mackerel was near. The dolphins swam to the mackerel and began to catch fish to eat. What a party it was! They ate and played and whistled to one another as they swam underwater.

Then one dolphin gave a sharp whistle and a crack. That meant "Danger!"

A small shark was swimming toward them. He seemed only to want some of the mackerel, so the dolphins let him alone. The shark ate a few mackerel and then swam away.

In late November, when the little dolphin was almost seven months old, a bad storm blew over the water. The wind pushed the waves higher and higher. The sun was hidden behind dark clouds. Thunder rumbled, and lightning cracked.

The little dolphin was frightened, so she swam close to her mother's side. There she felt safe from the storm. Mother Dolphin patted her with a flipper and showed her how to ride the ocean waves. They stayed close together underwater during the storm. As she swam with her mother, the little dolphin could hear the sound of the raindrops on the ocean water. Once, when she lifted her blowhole above the water for air, a raindrop fell into it. She coughed until she could breathe again.

At last the storm ended. The clouds rolled

away, and the sun set like a golden ball in the sky. The wind still blew, and the dolphins swam up and down with the waves. It was almost like being rocked in a big cradle. Then the moon rose above the dark water. The dolphins whistled as they talked to one another. Some napped while others talked. They would never go into a deep sleep, for they always had to push their blowholes above water to breathe.

Not far away, a hungry tiger shark was swimming. He was an ugly fellow, nearly ten feet long. His body was lean and striped. His tail moved from side to side as he swam along looking for food. His pale eyes looked about. His mouth was open, and his sharp teeth were ready to bite.

The tiger shark moved closer and closer to

the school of dolphins. He picked out the little dolphin. The dolphins would have heard the shark if they hadn't been napping and whistling. Even The Hunter didn't hear the shark until it was too late.

Tiger sharks kill many dolphins each year.

Suddenly, the Hunter whistled loudly. But by that time the shark had made a deep cut in the little dolphin's side.

Mother Dolphin hit the tiger shark hard with her head. The Fighter swiftly hit the shark from the other side. The dolphins killed the shark, and his body sank to the bottom of the ocean.

Mother Dolphin knew that other sharks, far away, would soon smell the baby's blood in the water and come to find her. She knew she had to take the young one to a safer place. So Mother swam toward quiet water near the shore.

A scab soon formed over the cut in the little dolphin's side. But she was still very frightened. She made whimpering sounds and swam very close to Mother Dolphin.

When the sun started to climb up in the sky, the little dolphin saw the white sand of a beach for the first time. She saw big trees beyond the sand. Mother Dolphin caught a fish between her teeth and tossed it to the little one. But the little dolphin didn't catch the fish this time. She still was too frightened to want to eat. Instead, she swam to her mother's underside and drank some milk.

Just then, two young men put a net into a small boat near shore. They were going out to catch some fish. They turned on the boat's engine, and the boat sped through the water.

One of the men saw Mother Dolphin and the little one. He turned down the engine until the boat was hardly moving through the water.

"Look," he said to his friend. "A mother

dolphin is bringing her little one close to shore. That usually means the baby dolphin is sick or hurt."

"Maybe we can help them," the friend said.

The boat moved closer to the dolphins. The young men could see the long cut the tiger shark had made in the little dolphin's side.

One of the young men slid from the boat into the water. He swam close to the dolphins but did not try to touch them. Mother Dolphin and the little one watched him. They could see that he did not want to hurt them. The young man swam back to the boat, and the dolphins followed him. The young man got the fishing net and put it under the little dolphin. She was quiet and still as the men lifted her into the boat. Both men took off their shirts and dipped them in the salt water. They put the

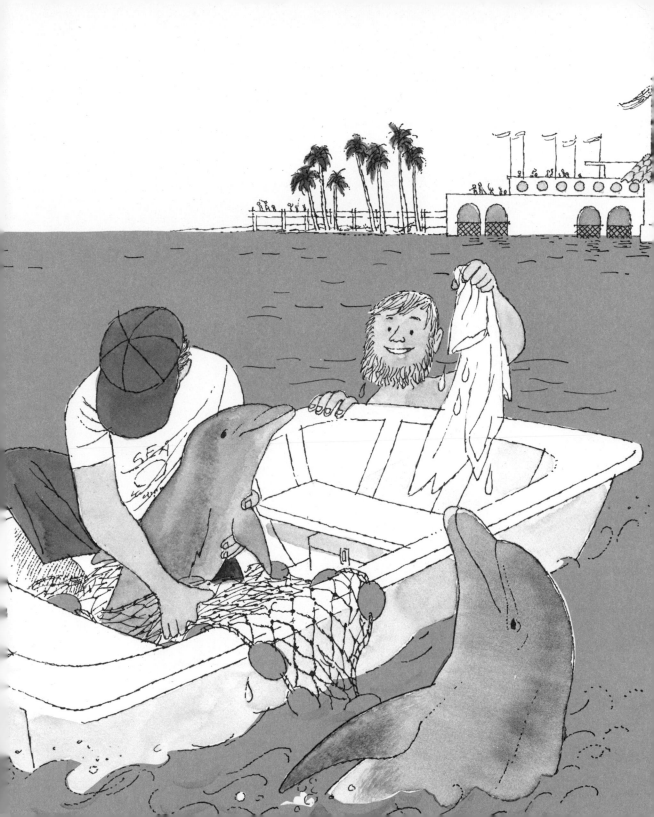

wet shirts over the little dolphin to keep her skin damp. They were careful not to cover the blowhole on top of her head.

The young men worked for a nearby sea show that had many dolphins. They knew the doctor who took care of the other dolphins could help the little one.

Mother Dolphin swam beside the boat as the young men started for the dock. One of the men called the sea show office on his two-way radio. He asked for the doctor to meet them at the door.

By the time the doctor arrived, the little dolphin looked very sick. Her eyes were half-closed. Her blowhole was opening and closing very fast, as if she were breathing hard.

The doctor looked her over carefully. "The cut in her side is already healing," he said. "I think she's just frightened now. She'll be all right."

Next to the dock was a big gate that opened into the holding pen for dolphins. One of the men opened the gate. The other man drove the boat through the opening. Mother Dolphin swam beside them. The men lifted the little dolphin out of the boat and put her in the water. She swam close to Mother Dolphin.

The holding pen was a large saltwater pool. Five other bottle-nosed dolphins were swimming there. They whistled to the mother and her little one. They told the mother not to let the little one swim too close to the side of the pool. She might scrape her skin against it. They knew the mother and baby had always lived in the big ocean, where there were no side walls.

Soon the five dolphins began to whistle to one another. They clacked their teeth in excitement. They could hear the footsteps of the man who would bring them fish. It was time to eat!

The man stood at the side of the pool with two big buckets filled with fish. He threw a fish to the biggest of the five dolphins, and the big dolphin leaped high in the air to catch it. He threw fish to all five of the dolphins, and they clacked their teeth for more.

Then he threw fish to Mother Dolphin and the little one. They did not try to catch the fish. They were used to catching their own fish in the ocean. They did not want to eat fish thrown from a bucket.

The little dolphin drank her mother's milk, but Mother Dolphin ate nothing at all. Mother

Dolphin ate nothing the next day or the day after that. The little dolphin drank milk. Even though the little one had learned to like fish, she would still drink her mother's milk until she was more than a year old.

On the third night, Mother Dolphin heard something. She swam to the gate that opened into the ocean. The little dolphin swam with her. Far away, under the water, they could hear dolphin sounds. They heard the name-whistle of Father Dolphin. They heard the whistles of The Hunter, The Fighter, and the others in the school of dolphins.

Mother Dolphin gave her name-whistle. She let the others know that the little dolphin was safe and well. She and the little one could hear the others whistle to them as they swam away.

The next morning Mother Dolphin and the little one ate their fish when the man fed them. Then they splashed and played with the other dolphins.

That afternoon, the man opened a gate at the end of the holding pen. One by one, the five dolphins swam through the gate into a narrow chute. Mother Dolphin and the little one followed them. The chute led to a big saltwater swimming pool that was 30 feet deep and nearly 100 feet long. Around the sides of the pool were rows of benches filled with people. It was time for the sea show!

At first, Mother Dolphin and the little one swam by themselves near one side of the pool. They watched as a man tossed a ball to one of the dolphins. It caught the ball and then tossed it back.

The man climbed onto a little platform over the water and held a fish high above his head. Another dolphin leaped into the air and took the fish from his hand.

The little dolphin and her mother watched. This was like their games in the ocean with the school of dolphins. The man held a big hoop over the water. One by one, the five

dolphins jumped through the hoop. Then Mother Dolphin jumped through the hoop, too. The little one tried, but she couldn't jump high enough. She fell back into the water with a splash. The crowd cheered, for most of the people had never seen a young dolphin.

Just then, a strong wind blew a little girl's hat from her head. The hat flew through the air. Mother Dolphin caught the hat and tossed it to the little one. The little dolphin caught the hat on her head. All the people laughed at the smiling little dolphin with a hat on her head. The little dolphin tried to stand on her tail, as she had tried so many times in the ocean. She almost made it.

"She looks just like a dolphin doll!" cried a woman.

The man on the platform said, "That's what we'll call her—Doll, the Dolphin!"

Then he tried to get the little girl's hat back. Doll wanted to keep it. But, finally, she swam close and let the man lift the hat from her head. The hat was wet from the water in the pool. The man gave it back to the little girl. He told her that she could have a free ticket to another sea show for letting the dolphin wear the hat.

Once more, the little dolphin tried to stand on her tail. The man gave her a fish. Then he

These bottle-nosed
dolphins
are acting
in sea shows
in Florida.

opened the gate to the holding pen. One by one, the dolphins swam back to the pen through the chute.

The next day the man came to play with Doll. He had two toys for her. He got into the water with one toy in his hand. It was a little rubber hat that floated on the water.

At first, he tossed the hat into the air so Doll could catch it on her head. Then he tossed the hat to Doll on the water. Doll swam under the hat and came up with it on her head.

When Doll was tired of that game, the man put the hat away. Then he brought out the other toy. It was a big blue hoop. He held the hoop above the water and called, "Jump, Doll!" She didn't understand the words, but she knew he wanted her to jump through the hoop. She jumped through it the first time! He

held the hoop a little higher. She jumped through it again! The man knew that soon the little one would be strong enough to jump even higher.

Doll was very happy. That night, as she swam near her mother, she gave a little whistle. Then she gave another whistle. Finally, she surprised even herself. She gave a special whistle that wasn't like any whistle she had ever heard before.

Mother Dolphin swam around her, whistling and splashing. The other dolphins whistled, too. Then they were quiet as Doll the Dolphin once more tried the special whistle. It was her name-whistle! At last, she had a name-whistle of her own, a sound she could make whenever she wanted to tell another dolphin who she was!

# Index

**Atlantic Ocean,** 1 (map), 5

**Blowhole(s),** 5, 7, 17-18, 24

**Bottle-nosed dolphins**
  birth, 6 (pic)
  communication, 7-11, 12, 15, 18-20,
    25, 28, 38
  description, 5
  enemies, 7, 11, 15, 20
  food and feeding, 8, 9 (pic), 11,
    14-15, 21, 26 (pic), 27-29
  game playing, 12-14
  mating, 5
  school, herd, 11-14, 28

**Sea show(s),** 24, 30-31 (pics), 30-33,
  34-35 (pics), 40 (pic)

**Sharks (tiger),** 18-20